I Am a Mute Iraqi with a Voice

Weam Namou

HERMiZ
PUBLiSHING

Hermiz Publishing, Inc.

Copyright © 2015 by Weam Namou

All rights reserved. No part of this book may be reproduced or transmitted in any form or by any means, electronic or mechanical, including photocopying, recording or by any information storage and retrieval system, without permission from the author.

Library of Congress Cataloging-in-Publication Data

2 0 1 5 9 0 7 1 3 7

Namou, Weam
I Am a Mute Iraqi with a Voice (poetry)
ISBN 978–0-9752956–9-4 (paperback)

First Edition

Published in the United States of America by:
Hermiz Publishing, Inc.
Sterling Heights, MI

This book is dedicated to the poetry group that
Pat Rozyski invited me to join in the 1990s.
A special thanks to Elisabeth Khan, not only a member
of that group but also the editor of this book.

Contents

Acknowledgments   viii
Introduction   x

PART I War, War, War
The Midwife of Fallujah   1
Miriam   3
I Am a Mute Iraqi with a Voice   5
The Sky is Brown   7
The Guilt I Feel   9
My Condolences, Iraq . . .   10
American and Iraqi Soldiers Unite in a Dance   11
Operation Iraqi Freedom Enslaved Me   13
The Dogs in America Live Better Than Us   14
The Wild Adventures of War   16
Hitting on Girls Overseas   18
Bread and Blood in the Streets of Baghdad   20
Dear Iraq   22
The Asian Cup   23

PART II: Countries, Memories and Veils
That Line   26
America   27
Remembering a Childhood in Iraq   28
Love, Justice, and Turtle Soup   30
What Stands Between Us   32

The Veil of Vanilla and Fire   33
Criticizing Trees   35
Punctuations and Montage   36
Tangerines, Shipped to Europe from Tangier 38
The Big Guys 40
From Baghdad to Times Square   42
That to That   44
My Beautiful Barbaric Land   45
Fleeing Saddam   46
Dressing Differently   48
An Unhealthy Relationship   49

PART III: Life and Family
My Brother's Wife   52
Pomegranate 53
It Was Supposed to Rain Today   55
A Mentor   57
The Bead Ceremony 58
I am a writer   59
Talking to My Birth Country 60
Why She's Unaware   61
My Company 62
Progress Trap 63
Expecting   64
What I Remember About Paris   66
A Letter Addressed to Me   68
Earthenware   70
The Five of Us   71

Our Bride   72
My Power Song   73
My Sunshine's First Day of School   74
A Waitress and a Nun   76
What a Morning   77
A Season's Breeze   78
A Step Backward to Move Forward   79
He and I   80
The Idea of Positivity   81
My Pencil   82
A Memory of Mother   84
Traveling Abroad Without Leaving Town   86
Both Without Teeth   87
Sense and Humor   88
Before We Get Married   89
Similarities   91
Dear Mother   92
My Little Woman   93
My Brother   94
The Mistress   95
Original Birth   96

PART IV: Animals and Vegetables
At the Dog Mall   98
Diego by the Pool   100
Planting Life   102
The Polish Rooster   103
Like Prophets and Saints   105

I Am a Mute Iraqi with a Voice

Termites   106
Pomme   107
A Butterfly   108
Fish   109
Spring is Here 110

Acknowledgments

Some of the poems in this book first appeared in the following publications, sometimes in a slightly different form:

The Midwife of Fallujah
- Published in a chapbook by *Lettre Sauvage* as part of a collection of poems for the Al Mutanabbi Street Project

Miriam
Dear Iraq
World Literature Today (November/December 2007)

I Am a Mute Iraqi with a Voice
The Wild Adventures of War
Bread and Blood in the Streets of Baghdad
Poets Against War

The Sky Is Brown
November 3rd Club (Fall 2009)

American and Iraqi Soldiers Unite in a Dance
My Brother's Wife
Glass: A Journal of Poetry (Volume one Issue Three—December 2008)

That Line
Acumen 59 (September 2007)

America
[Remembering] a Childhood in Iraq
Mascara Literary Review (January 2011)

I Am a Mute Iraqi with a Voice

Love, Justice, and Turtle Soup
What Stands Between Us
SNR Review

The Veil of Vanilla and Fire
Gargoyle: Issue 56

Criticizing Trees
*Folly Magazine (*March 2010)

Pomegranate
Arab World Books

It Was Supposed to Rain Today
Progress Trap
Danse Macabre (Volume Five, Number Nine)

A Mentor
Pea River Journal (February 2013)

Why She's Unaware
My Company
Mizna Literary Journal (Volume 9, Issue 2, 2007)

What I Remember About Paris
River Poets Journal (Winter 2010)

Tangerines, Shipped to Europe from Tangier
Gloom Cupboard (November 2009)

A Letter Addressed to Me
Silenced Press (August 2009)

Introduction

When I had my first child nine years ago, I thought I would have to give up writing until she started preschool. I had by then written three novels and, given the demands of motherhood, I knew I could not easily formulate on paper a dozen sentences, let alone a 300 page manuscript. Then one day, while my daughter was taking her nap, I sat on the couch with a pen and paper and wrote a story through a poem. This was not my first poem.

I wrote my first poem in 2001 when I attended the Prague Summer Seminar that was sponsored by the University of New Orleans. Before that, poetry was as foreign to me as Baghdad is to westerners. Studying a new form of writing in such a structurally beautiful and strikingly colorful city proved to be quite natural. I would grab a coffee and croissant every morning from a local café, head to Charles University, founded in 1348, and sit in a classroom taught by American poet Anne Marie Macari. I listened to poetry readings by the late, renowned Czech author Arnost Lustig and Pulitzer Prize winner Philip Levine. I enjoyed plenty of goulash, strolls down Charles Bridge, and walks on park trails lined with pear trees.

The experience in Prague filled me with a love for poetry, but I did not start writing poems again until six years later, when I became a mother. My creativity found an outlet through this language and my soul collected joy as I placed literature on paper in between cooking a curry stew or while cartoons held my children's attention. Within a poem, I discovered I could share an intimacy with literature without the pressure and length of time that a novel required. It was like enjoying a meal with a loved one. You give those moments your time and energy and then each one goes their separate way. With a novel, you feel attached at the hip for a year or two.

Over the next ten years, I managed to return to writing 300-plus-page manuscripts, memoirs this time. But my love for poetry has always remained. I believe it was always in me, it was in my genes. When I read about my ancestors, the ancient Mesopotamians, who invented writing, the image of Enheduanna always comes to mind.

Enheduanna is the world's first recorded writer. She was the daughter of the great Mesopotamian king Sargon of Akkad and the high priestess of the temple of Nanna, the Akkadian moon god, in the center of her father's empire, the city state of Ur. She had a considerable political and religious role in Ur. She wrote during the rise of the agricultural civilization when gathering territory and wealth, warfare, and patriarchy were making their marks. She offers a first-person perspective on the last times women in western society held religious and civil power.

After her father's death, the new ruler of Ur removed her from her position as high priestess. She turned to the goddess Inanna to regain her position, through a poem that mentions her carrying the ritual basket:

*"It was in your service that I first entered the holy temple,
I, Enheduanna, the highest priestess. I carried the ritual basket,
I chanted your praise.
Now I have been cast out to the place of lepers.
Day comes and the brightness is hidden around me. Shadows cover the light, drape it in sandstorms.
My beautiful mouth knows only confusion.
Even my sex is dust."*

Enheduanna lived at a time of rising patriarchy. It has been written that as secular males acquired more power, religious beliefs had evolved from what was probably a central female deity in Neolithic times to a central male deity by the Bronze Age. Female power and freedom sharply diminished during the Assyrian era, the period in which the first evidence of laws requiring veiling of elite women in public was made.

I Am a Mute Iraqi with a Voice is my first poetry book in honor of my ancestors.

PART I

War, War, War

The Midwife of Fallujah

Everyone knew *Amti* Hassina, a Christian,
who lived alone in Fallujah
after her husband went missing in some war
and left her to raise a little boy.

The midwife and nurse of the city of mosques and history
which was inhabited for many millennia,
most recently by those of Sunni ancestry,
Amti Hassina was called upon by all.

Repaid with money, live chickens, fresh eggs, dried dates
and figs, she lived like a queen, although there, she wasn't
linked by lineage.

I never met *Amti* Hassina's patients in real life nor in pictures.
But last night I think I did and they cut apart my heart.

These images might be graphic, warned the Internet.
Still, I clicked the mouse on all seventy-two of them.
I couldn't eat my pita club sandwich afterward
but I had to view or else it meant no recognition for
the tormented.

I thanked *Allah* Aunt Hassina wasn't around
to see Fallujah an empty ground,

to weep over men and women she might've once treated,
or given birth to, lying in their beds,
swimming in their blood, faces blown off,
hair and skin scalded, bodies partially eaten
by dogs, birds and cats.

Miriam

Named after the Virgin Mary,
born in an Arabic land,
Miriam is the newest cousin in our family.
She is eight months younger than my daughter
who lives thousands of miles away across the ocean
on American ground.

This June Miriam will experience her first summer.
I wonder how that will be.
Last year her pregnant mother suffered tremendously–
her grandfather too—from the lack of water and electricity
in Baghdad's unbearable humidity.

How do these people survive, I wonder,
when pretty much all day they're forced to remain inside?
What will this baby see when she starts to understand?
Nothing, I'm afraid, but a crumbled sorrowful land.

She will hear stories by her ancestors
who'll describe to her the wonders of her once beautiful
land when they were able to sit on the porch,
drink tea, listen to Abd Al-Haleem Hafiz and laugh;
when boys and girls played safely in the streets
and at the end of the day fell sound asleep,
maybe once in a while being woken by a nightmare.

But never—no, not in the good old days—
by the sound of explosives, shotguns
and women's unbearable weeping.

I Am a Mute Iraqi with a Voice

I am an Iraqi
but was never asked personally,
what was better?
Saddam threatening to destroy me if I crossed him politically,
or tons of depleted uranium, napalm,
bullets, explosives
and other unfamiliar concoctions besieging me
at some hidden corner of my street?

I am an Iraqi
but was never asked personally,
what I wanted?
Freedom to vote for men and women I know little about,
who may or may not better my life,
or to be able to safely step out of my house?

I am an Iraqi
but was never asked,
do I want democracy
or the tradition of my ancestry?

I am an Iraqi
but was never asked personally,
by those who've come to rescue me,
Have we really benefited you, my dear,

since the day we came near?
Or have we simply made a mess
of your little hut?

The Sky is Brown

My hair is white
from the sand
that burns my eyes
if I don't wear glasses.

The water kept in tanks
is scorching hot due to the
120-degree temperatures
all summer long.

The water from
the well is bitter and salty
and needs boiling prior to
swallowing.

Last time it rained
was nine months ago,
the time it takes for a woman
to carry full term.

Weather is so bad here
it makes me want to vomit.

Baghdad is not the same.
One never sees a star.

The sky is dark brown.
No gardens.
Just tensions.

I came here to interpret for the U.S. Army.
The economy at home is bad.
The pay here is good.
I could die at any moment.

The Guilt I Feel

The guilt I feel in America
to be able to put my daughter in
a stroller and walk around the block,
get a little exercise and some fresh air
while relatives in my birth country of Iraq
hide indoors, avoid God's breeze,
as it may contain fire and ashes,
perhaps drops of blood and words of hatred.

The guilt I feel in America
when I go all day with electricity,
water, as well as the ability to
have no curfew or weaponry
near my front porch or backyard
while relatives in my birth country of Iraq
buy radiators, if they can afford them,
boil water in the winter to have a nice bath
and in the summer,
if their child has a fever,
have him or her lie on the cold tile floor
to cool off as a method of cure.

The guilt I feel in America
because my taxes paid for other women
and children to live in constant lack and fear.

My Condolences, Iraq . . .

I asked a man who's stationed
in Iraq, "How is Iraq?"
He said, "My condolences to Iraq."

I jotted down this important note
and thought it wise to quickly tell the U.S.A.
that Iraq is dead, they need no longer fret.

What should be done now is to praise
the deceased, to finally remember her
beauty and accomplishments.

Now that Iraq has died, we can talk
about how she once was a happy land,
the cradle of civilization.

Perhaps I can pass on this information
at the rally in Downtown Detroit,
being held for those who died last week in a church in Iraq,
killed by six terrorists who entered the
holy place and shot away for five hours straight
while hundreds of "security" stood outside,
twiddling their thumbs and discussing politics.

American and Iraqi Soldiers Unite in a Dance

It's a sophisticated dance,
needing the finesse of a jeweler's hands,
which cuts a diamond into
this and that shape at a future bride's demands.

People's fingers interlock in this ancient dance,
forming a circle as large as a farmer's land
while they move in unison to the melody and rhythm of a
tambourine, dumbek and bamboo flute.

The *debke* is a community dance for Middle Easterners–
each region, from Syria to Lebanon, having its own structure
and design– often performed at weddings and other joyous
occasions. Recently a new group has emerged to join its
natural movements.

I saw them on TV. They were celebrating in Kurdistan which
is north of Iraq.
American and Iraqi soldiers, grouped side by side,
dressed in khaki, holding hands as if they were one family.

American soldiers having adopted and mastered that?
Two countries, thinking they're worlds apart, are coinciding

Weam Namou

and recognizing the benefit and bliss of uniting.

Is there possibly a happy ending to this war story?
Do these lands have a calling?
Will one day my birth country of Iraq
and my home of America
be crowned with the term, "They lived happily ever after?"
Let's wait and see and pray for that.

Operation Iraqi Freedom Enslaved Me

Do you realize what has happened to me?
If I tell you, could you possibly understand?
I, who once dressed as I pleased and went out on the streets to attend class, visit my neighbors, or buy apples and tangerines from the fruit market stand, am no longer able to set foot outside of my home without the fear of being kidnapped, raped, tortured or killed, just because I am wearing makeup or a cross, or not veiled, or simply because I am female.

Even in my home I am not safe
from the civil war that has come knocking on our door
due to the people who believed they were giving my
sisters and me all sorts of freedoms and liberties.
Do they realize now that what they have actually done
is bring along artillery and thousands of terrorists,
all of which have done a pretty good job enslaving me?

The Dogs in America Live Better Than Us

Once upon a time, during that very first war,
I came to your home and
for 42 of the harshest winter days,
dropped over 88,000 tons of bombs
on your territory, thus putting your people in total dismay.

I cut off your water and electricity supply,
caused acute shortages of food, even medicines,
offered only remorseless bombing around the clock,
ignored the stories of pregnant women having to give birth
in the dark without anyone to help but the Lord whose name
I used going into this bloody fight.

During the sanctions that lasted for twelve years,
I listened as non-profit organizations told me that
women were watching their infants die of malnutrition
and disease, and in 2001, I saw with my own two eyes how
children were being killed indirectly, the way it happens
with unfed flies.

During this most current war,
I've watched daily on TV the turmoil I cause the men,
women and children of a country

I Am a Mute Iraqi with a Voice

I have successfully taken backwards hundreds of centuries. I feel so guilty that, thanks to me, many Iraqis have said, "The dogs in America live better than us."

The Wild Adventures of War

So many of my friends now dead,
killed by insurgents who ripped apart
their cross and stabbed them in the heart.
Or by U.S. soldiers who mistook them for bad women
and men, not ordinary civilians.

So many relatives attacked right in their homes
by men wearing hoods, holding guns and shouting out their
creed. These families have had to flee due to those horrible
fears which they never experienced from anyone,
not even from Saddam's *wazirs*.

I should do what's customary, tear out my hair in grieving,
but I myself wonder how I will survive this nightmare that's
so horrendous. After all, I could get blown up any second
while walking or driving on Baghdad's streets.
Or my home may receive bullets or a grenade while I try
to decide if I ought to cook okra or curry stew.

Plus I must find new ways to tolerate the summer and
winter of Baghdad when all we get is one to two hours of
electricity a day and so little water, it's barely enough to
wash our tears away. Am I again to bear it as I yearly do,

just fan my face with cardboard while eating sunflower seeds, staring at my fate and feeling blue?

All this trouble I can no longer swallow.
And yet I must also be irked by the lack of gas in my husband's car tank since right now there's close to zero oil in my country, even though that is the number-one resource in our industry. But I swear there have been days when my husband had run out of gas and finding no other ride, ended up sleeping in his truck.

Oh well, these are the wild adventures of war. What else was I expecting to get –
rose petals, fancy shoes, and cheese fondues?

Hitting on Girls Overseas

This is Baghdad.
This is a merchant street.
These are young, dark and handsome men who hang out during tea time and observe the females that happen to pass by. "That's a real nice cart," they will say
about the women with attractive behinds.
One day one woman responded,
"Would you like to be my mule and draw this cart
which you seem to like?"

This is Baghdad.
This is a different merchant street.
The same young, dark and handsome men who hang out during tea time continue to observe the females that happen to pass by and when a pregnant woman wobbles by,
they enunciate, "She has been stung by a bee!"
to which one day a woman retorted,
"Would you like my bee to sting you too?"

This is Baghdad.
This is yet another merchant street.
The same dark and handsome men who hang out during tea time cannot find any females to hit on.

I Am a Mute Iraqi with a Voice

The neighborhoods are empty of their kind
because this is Baghdad
after the invasion,
after the kidnappings,
killings
and rapes!

Bread and Blood in the Streets of Baghdad

The sister of my husband,
my second cousin Hind.
In Arabic that translates to India
but she lives in Baghdad, north of what once was Babylonia.

She walks outside in her memory.
She prays at home for her family,
certain her land will never recover
from the turmoil of bombs, rapes, kidnappings,
all sorts of troubles.

She doesn't leave her home
for fear she will disappear,
the way her church turned into rubble
and a civilian nearby was frozen into ash.

She sweeps the sand from the previous night's storm
and as she suffocates within the four brick walls,
asks God that her brother returns safely home
so she wouldn't regret having sent him for bread.

I listen to her describe her sorrows and heaviness.
I'm unable to give any false promises
that her situation will improve.
She knows better than I, anyway, that there is no cure.

I Am a Mute Iraqi with a Voice

"You have one minute remaining."

The famous U.S. phone card with the picture of a herd of camels and a jeep is at its end, as are the hearts of the Iraqis who've suffered the Gulf War, followed by the sanctions, followed by Operation: Iraqi Freedom,
by all those oppressive attempts at liberation.

Dear Iraq

Dear Iraq,

They have made a mess out of you
while I and others watched, like tombs.

But what could we do?
Voting didn't help, nor protesting.

Not showing your dying children on TV
nor placing horrific war pictures on the web.

We stood still and watched
and were torn apart
between the land of our hopes and dreams
and the one of our sweet childhood memories.

The Asian Cup

Today you lost, dear Iraqi team,
who, due to your dire conditions,
play soccer as a way to distill the tears
and to envision there are no battlefields
in your neighborhood streets.

Today you lost
after having enjoyed the championship
for the very first time last year
and having made it to the final playoff game
five years following the invasion, this horrific war
whose intentions, until now, are left unclear.

Today you lost
and therefore no one linked to your country
can celebrate, go out into the streets,
beep horns, dance and scream
like they did the same time last year.
Instead, they feel sad again
as has become the custom of Iraqis' daily lives.

Today you lost
which means there will be fewer bombings
in cafes and in the market place
as the insurgents will be happy of your defeat.

Weam Namou

And that's one of the positives,
what we in America call the bright side of things.

So while you have not won the Asian cup,
your loss might possibly have saved some lives–
children, women, men and the elderly–
who would've otherwise paid a dear price for your victory!

PART II

Countries, Memories and Veils

That Line

Who casts the vote on where the east and north end,
and the south and west begin?
Where is that line?
I search for it and wonder
if it's pink, gold, silver, charcoal, or chocolate.
Does it feel like pebbles, sand, lipstick, chalk or rain?

I left Saddam airport, had my passport stamped in blue ink,
crossed over lands, jungles, farms, and oceans,
saw the Statue of Liberty before I flew into Detroit
and drove on Highway 94, passing by that big tire
until I arrived at my new residence.
But nowhere did I detect a trace of that line.

Where is that line that is as perfectly drawn on the map
as the decorations of a wedding cake
or the hem on my blouse and skirt?
If it's not visible on soil and grass,
how am I expected to grasp it in my head?
Should I force myself to pretend it's alive, not dead?

Regardless of what is written or said,
lines do not exist in one's soul.
They have no place in the heart.
They cannot bring other countries closer or push them apart.

America

I talk about you, as many others do,
sticking labels such as *arrogant* and *gullible*
over your name, like stamps on a large Christmas package.

You dress me with possibilities,
I try on this and that outfit of different colors and sizes,
meanwhile focusing on your limitations.

You do not reprimand me for my verbal thoughts.
Rather, you listen, weigh the options
and consider whether what I have to say is worthy of action.

Oftentimes, I even receive applause
for pointing out your negativities and idiocies. In return,
you remain true to the First Amendment you've provided.

You've allowed me to take a deep look at your weaknesses
and in turn caused me to appreciate your strength and
integrity. That's real balance, the yin and yang, of our planet.

While I love the country of my birth, Iraq,
where I was blessed with the best childhood,
I must admit, had I remained there as an adult,
Freedom of Speech is something I might never have
experienced.

Remembering a Childhood in Iraq

Sun shines over a mélange of
green grass and white snow,
like a lime-flavored Slurpee.
Snow was rarely detected in Baghdad.

Through the window a squirrel
passes by, nibbles at the cereal
I've left for it on the deck.
Pets are not encouraged in Iraq.

A lunch of hot tea and a cold slice
of pepperoni pizza I prepare for me,
without removing the pepperoni.
Pork is not *halal* in the Arab world.

I listen to the poetic Quranic verses on TV
even though I belong to a Christian minority
who still speak Aramaic, called the Chaldeans.
They're being persecuted in their native land as we speak.

All praise is due to Allah, Lord of the Worlds . . .
the imam leads a prayer.
I remember the paper bag of baby green apples
my father used to bring home for us.

I Am a Mute Iraqi with a Voice

My younger brother and I tied
their stems to a string,
treated the apples like yoyos.
We had no toys back then, nor swings.

We built play houses out of cardboard boxes,
pretended pillows were our dolls,
pots and utensils our musical instruments.
In Iraq, today, children can't afford to be that simple.

We needed no one to read us a bedtime story:
aunts and uncles, cousins and neighbors
were our heroes and villains.
Now, terrorists and gangs rule that part of the earth.

Love, Justice, and Turtle Soup

A Native American man with long hair
walked into my place of business one day
and verbally handed me a recipe,
though I did not cook at the time,
and now that I do cook, I doubt
I could follow the instructions he gave to me,
though I'll never forget the recipe.

He said, nonchalantly:

"If you want to make homemade turtle soup, you have to be careful and you must wait. You'd want to catch a sea turtle because you get thirty or more pounds of meat from it—depending on size. You need help, too. A couple of men would do, to place the turtle inside a garbage can filled with fresh water. Close the lid and leave it there to starve.

It sounds brutal, I know, but there's no other way to do it if you want to have homemade turtle soup. Sea turtles can live up to a hundred years, so it takes a while for them to die. If someone tried to slaughter them, they'd release a poison into their system that would kill anyone who ate their meat. One must therefore keep the area surrounding the garbage can quiet so the turtle doesn't think it has been caught by anyone but itself . . . Turtles have a bad memory and will forget they were trapped."

I Am a Mute Iraqi with a Voice

People trap each other like that and call it love.

Elephants, on the other hand, don't forget.
If someone tried to hurt them, they come back after a hundred years to step on them.

People avenge each other like that and call it justice.

What Stands Between Us

A book.
Yes, a book—two, or three, to be exact—
of differences and similarities:
The Torah, the Bible and the Quran.

Followers of each are offended by the other,
though they are sisters and brothers.
They try to prove their points
and in the midst of their dispute,
they scream and shout,
surely upsetting their Father Abraham.

"Don't hit, share!" they teach their kids
while the leaders of their nations not only hit,
but kill.

The Veil of Vanilla and Fire

While visiting my parents' Christian
village in Iraq, I bought an *abaya,*
known around the world as a veil,
a symbol that has since 9/11 become
the enemy of democracy.

Some may say the veil reminds them of ninjas,
of burglars or other scary sights;
they may also philosophize that veils represent
oppression, fundamentalism and other negative vibes.
Myself, I have a different memory of this piece of cloth.

When I was a little girl, I used my mother's
veil to play house. She and the neighborhood
women wore it for various purposes:

Convenience
to remain in their nightgown as they visited the *souk* or bakery.
Concealment
to meet a lover or pursue other private affairs without anyone's recognition.
Modesty
due to their culture and religion.
Beautification
the attractive manner in which it flutters around the waist

and ankle gave it style.

I couldn't wait to grow up and have my own veil,
not knowing then that one day
wearing fabric in such a manner,
or not wearing it,
could cost women their lives.

Criticizing Trees

I criticize the veil you wear.
You criticize the two-piece bathing suit
I have on, customs that are not really our own,
some of which have been bestowed upon us
by men's desires and jealousies.

Since childhood, we've been told
that we stem from one Woman, Adam's partner.
Yet we treat each other like rivals, not kin,
forgetting the individual inside these petty clothes,
the one who cooks and cleans and does laundry,
she who toils for her family
does not place society's fashion as her priority,
regardless of whether she lives in Saudi Arabia or France,
is a resident of Miserable Island in Tasmania
or the Happy Town of Texas.

Look at birds and trees.

Punctuations and Montage

I attend a lecture by a screenwriter.

Watch the punctuation and question marks.
Must have conflict and resolution.

The audience dreams of writing the next great American movie. Some admit they do not have the talent or discipline to write.

The attention span of horror-movie goers is only ninety minutes. Kids can't even last that long . . .
Filmmakers have come up with a solution:
Ten minute montage with ten minutes of rolling credits.

Horror films are the most popular film genre. How scary is that?

What I discovered as I'm writing a novel that takes place in 1896 is that what we were doing before and
what we're doing now is not the same.
But people are really the same.

Thought we'd evolved, to where people now-a-days enter gyms and schools and shoot point blank.

I Am a Mute Iraqi with a Voice

"Don't have a message.
People don't like to think."
Executives actually told me that.

Yet we believe that we are not oppressed by our surroundings.

Lecture is over.

I return home and write a poem, which may (God forbid) have a message to tell!

Tangerines, Shipped to Europe from Tangier

The name Tangerine comes from Tangier,
a city I visited long ago while in Morocco,
where different religions, even paganism, are accepted.
A group of veiled woman did snicker
at my sleeveless shirt . . .

I'm getting off track here.

Tangerines . . .if we could remove our
problems as easily as the peeling of this delicious fruit and
simply devour each slice to have
an unsolved issue disappear,
I would place each segment
in my mouth, and, prior to having anything resolved,
I'd visit the world I once had as a child in Baghdad,
the time before I ever knew the
difference between a Christian, Muslim or Jew,
had no idea what was the meaning of violence and crime.

What I do recall is that all the neighborhood women behaved
as though they were my mom. Daytime was for school:
I wore a uniform, sometimes navy other times grey.
My hair was in braids.
I took a lunch bag my mother had prepared.

I Am a Mute Iraqi with a Voice

Afternoons were for carefree play in the streets
with an ample supply of marbles and chalk,
jump rope, a carefully chosen square of rock
to use for hopscotch.

At night, I slept quite soundly,
maybe once or twice I was frightened by a ghost story.
I was told never to bring up Saddam's name
or talk to strangers or say the "A" word, i.e.
"America."

It was all so perfect
until we moved to America
in search of a better life
and discovered that a "better life" was not
served on a silver platter at the airport upon one's arrival.

Neither are problems resolved by the devouring of tangerines.

The Big Guys

Speak up!
Take action!
Sign a petition!
March and shout!
Do somersaults in front of the White House!
We absolutely must protest!

These are the messages we receive
since the attacks on Gaza have begun.
I do not approve of the violence that occurs
but I admit that I cannot move.
Forgive me for being pessimistic,
such an attitude is not tolerated in the West.
But let's forget optimism for a moment
and look at a little truth.

Despite all the attempts that were made to save it,
the entire country of Iraq has been destroyed,
brought down to rubble
turned into a dark and scary place.
No one would ever believe this land was
once the cradle of civilization,
the mother of science, reading and writing.

Now you want me to believe that my screams

I Am a Mute Iraqi with a Voice

and shouts will save a strip
that's half the size of Orange County?

We are like ants,
working hard,
collecting food,
eating whatever is made available out there,
marching to and fro,
building this sand castle and that, until a big foot
decides to step on us
because we are getting in his way
or merely because he is in the mood for play.

From Baghdad to Times Square

I'd lived in America for twenty years,
was no longer an immigrant but a full-fledged citizen.
And though I'd traveled the world quite a bit,
I was naïve enough to assume that
all the states in America resembled each other,
like bricks and concrete.

Then one day, I landed in Times Square
and witnessed the country which I often
saw in Baghdad, on the screen.
My siblings and I would huddle around,
eat sunflower seeds and whisper the word
"America," despite the fear that Saddam's men
might hear us through our thick barriers.

We were anxious to leave behind our old world,
what historians call the cradle of civilization,
and arrive at that intersection
full of people, lights, and street-vendor carts.
Yet what we saw upon landing in Michigan
were quiet areas called the suburbs.
No one was outside let alone walking or eating ice cream.

This was not the image we had in mind,
certainly not "Times Square,"

I Am a Mute Iraqi with a Voice

the mathematical name which reminds
me of Iraq, where the first school, map of the world,
and the idea of dividing time and space
into a multiple of 60's—the clock—were started.

In 1980, we left what once was the great empire of Babylon,
to share ourselves with the powerful Western Hemisphere,
the New World of today,
in order to experience what our ancestors
had practiced thousands of years ago,
a wealth of possibilities and the joys
of freedom and liberty.

That to That

I'm an immigrant who wonders,
Why do I have such resistance to my western land?

The fumes, city lights and traffic could fool one into believing
he's in Baghdad, Belgrade or any other downtown area.

They mean little on a map.
It's people who mark a country, the way cats do their owners.

Whether through veils or statues, they romance their
homeland with a history, their children with a lineage.

As with children, history should not be molded or possessed,
but rather, truly listened to.

I search for a way to release the grip I have of my past
without forgetting the spices and the sand
because I want to come to terms with what had brought
me here from the very beginning,
the words "freedom of speech and religion."

My Beautiful Barbaric Land

I come from a faraway land
that many consider barbaric
given that women there dress in veils
and their men have permission
to marry up to four females.

I come from a faraway land
that has a big soul, history and heart,
which very few can see or understand,
occupied as they may be with what
is being said on the television set.

I come from a faraway land
where a woman doesn't have the
pressure to be thin and a little
flesh here and there is a good sign.
Her weight issue belongs to her alone
and the word obesity does not exist so far.

I come from a faraway land
which is still called the cradle of civilization
because so much was discovered there,
was passed on to the rest of this earth,
to my new home, the youngest country known to mankind.

Fleeing Saddam

We want to run away
from Saddam and his
Baath regime and go to
America with the rest of our relatives.
They've lived there for years.

We got out of Iraq,
were smuggled to different countries.
In the boat that headed from
Turkey to Greece,
our newborn was given a pill
to sedate his cries
in order that none of us would be caught
for the smuggling crime.

We were happy to make it safely to Greece.
Our hopes were high.
No more dictatorship.
A new life was about to begin,
our family had been waiting a long time
for this monumental moment.

We felt like movie stars
as we neared the shores
of a European land.

I Am a Mute Iraqi with a Voice

We were free.
We could not believe our eyes.

"Honey, the baby is not breathing!"

Our nightmares re-began.

Dressing Differently

Yes, people dress differently around the world,
but a lot of that is about climate.
Berbers, for instance, have black tents
because the desert is hot in the daytime and cold at night.
There's no moisture in the air.

I listened to my teacher.

What distinguishes one person from another?
The name. It's at that point that the legend begins.
Power is contained in the name.
When the lineage is sung, names are mentioned,
ancestors remembered and all of a sudden
you belong to a community.
We see how we transcended and transformed.

I listened to my teacher.

You came to me for support, didn't you?
If you know something for sure,
you don't need support.
You need only understanding and companionship.

An Unhealthy Relationship

You lied to me when
you said I had freedom
of speech because each time I
speak freely,
I pay a price that silences me.

You lied to me when
you said justice and liberty for all
because oftentimes when I watch the news,
when I undergo scrutiny due to my opinions and
beliefs, I don't feel liberated, and I ask,
where's the justice in that?

Yet through all your deceptions
I value your good, your wanting
to be godlike.
And I love you.
I love your ideals and gullibility.
I love your desire to seek the truth.

Torn between you and my birthplace,
where do I go?
Which side do I take?
Why do I have to take sides?
Why can't I be free to not

take sides without being called un-American?

I am American. By choice.

PART III

Life and Family

My Brother's Wife

She brought along clothes, high heels, and gold
but no résumés or diplomas.
Her mastery was in her glance, her touch,
her movements.

Her name is Zina
Translation: decoration
She entered our home in autumn,
inhabited the fourth and largest chamber.

She fried tomatoes using extra care,
mopped each ceramic tile in fine detail,
climbed the stairs with passion,
looked at my brother with patience.

Watching her perform, I found surrender was her name.
Mine, intelligence.
She tiptoed closer to my space,
smelled disinterest and ran the other way.

One day she slipped in through the crack of my bedroom
door and gave me her dress to keep.
I wore it and recalled what it is to please.
I borrowed the depth of her life's embrace
then gave the dress to my sister.

Pomegranate

Some call it pomegranate,
others Indian apple.
Mother calls it *rumman*.

She slices it into halves
and serves it as though it were lamb
on a large silver tray with a floral design.

The children, chin within the tray's circle, bite into the fruit.
Crimson juice drips on the metal, tablecloth,
one's blouse, pajama sleeve, nightgown's ruffle.

Individual bits fall and get scooped up.
Hair strands are moved, curled around the ear while
beneath the chandelier, thin and full lips crunch and chew.

When all that's left are shells and peels,
red-stained hands reach for soap and water.
Everyone then lies on the rug, heel to heel.

They say, hmmm, how good that was,
point out who was messy, greedy,
complain that the boy's portions had more seeds,
were extra juicy.

Weam Namou

Hands inside the pockets of her summer dress,
mother lies, "To me, boy or girl—makes no difference."
With a smile, she walks away to her recess.

It Was Supposed to Rain Today

It was supposed to rain today
but it's warm and sunny instead.
I sit on the porch to have
my morning coffee, all alone,
with no one to call my name
to order apple juice or screech, "*boula*"
the Iraqi word for urine.

I've taken one, maybe two sips of my favorite drink,
Nescafé, a dash of sugar and milk,
when I hear the laughing voices
of my husband and daughter echo from inside the house.
He comes out, carrying her draped
over his shoulders like a sack of rice.

She is still in her pajamas, holding onto her blanket.

He instructs me to sit elsewhere:
There are bees in the barbecue grill beside me.
I move the chair to another place,
then do the same with my coffee cup,
the novel I'm reading, the journal I plan to write in,
the cell and home phones
I've taken outside so that
they will not wake up anyone when they ring.

He removes the cover of the barbecue grill.
Inside a honeycomb has been built.
A bright yellow bee comes to it.
I take a deep breath, close my eyes to pray.
"You're falling asleep!" I hear an elder warn.
I'm annoyed. It's an elder who is staying with us for a bit.

He brings over a scrub brush,
bangs the honeycomb, then the bee.
The honeycomb falls to the ground.
The bee is dead. A second bee flies away.

I pick up the honeycomb and observe there's no honey yet.
I think . . .of the people whose plans are spoiled
due to them being an inconvenience, or for whatever other reason, to another group of humans who are so mighty they can, with one bang, change the outcome of the weak ones' future.

A Mentor

Sometimes, a woman will appear out of nowhere,
from the mountains, desert, jungle or sky.
She is both young and old but she is not your mother, sister
or a peer. She sits in a circle and invites you for a cup of
tea. The moment you accept, she transforms into a goddess
who possesses an ancient soul, a sharp sense of humor and
red hair.

Before you have the chance to evaluate the situation,
you know her presence is sublime and you submit to
her design, recognizing she is here to teach you something,
hoping the mirror she holds up will deliver you from a rocky
path, a painful past.

This woman is full of wisdom, passion and fire and she
carries a bag of medicine for bad thoughts.
The medicine is made of feathers, rocks and sticks, has the
energy of eagles, dolphins and wolves. She brews her recipe
and sprinkles it over your head, pours it into your heart,
until you are stewed.

She does her magic and disappears
and you are left wondering, "What happened to our year?"

"I gave you what you needed," she says,
"I am now gone, but I am here."

The Bead Ceremony

My shaman teacher opened her hand and said,
"Take a bead for each one of your accomplishments."

Four glass beads decorated with pink roses
lay in the palm of her hand like Hershey's Kisses.
I took one, then another, then another.
Three is enough, appropriate.
I would not want to seem greedy
or overconfident or . . .

"Take the fourth one," she said. "You earned it."

She knew. She knew how hard I worked yearlong to cleanse my soul and mend the broken pieces of my dreams. She knew how difficult it was for me to reward myself appropriately.

I hugged her tight.

The ceremony was over but not the memory.
I revisit the experience each time
my fingers touch the slip pocket in my purse,
feeling the smoothness of the four beads
that represent my accomplishments, my family of four and
the four directions of the Native American wheel.

I am a writer

I am a writer.
Wherever I travel I pack
words, poems and stories
in a purse that's in my head.

This purse is crowded with
napkins, scrap paper, ticket stubs.
It's bursting with words.
Poems and stories fall here and there.
I try to pick them up and
stuff them back into the purse,
worrying that some have been lost forever.

I do my best to contain these
words, poems, stories.
They are precious to me.
But my purse bulges in pain,
unable to keep the zipper zipped,
the snap closed, the fabric of the purse intact.
They want out, to pour over the world
and touch people's hearts.

They beg to be released and I take a
pen and paper and, one by one,
release them through computer ink.

Talking to My Birth Country

I've traveled so far away from you Iraq
but yet I never fully left you.
You are in my daughter's and son's eyes,
my children who have never met you.

Our bodies and minds move from here to there
and back again, exploring new territories and
yet our souls, no matter how hard we may try,
do not release us from our past.

So when my daughter dips bread in olive oil and *zaatar,*
and my son wants his favorite egg and tomato sandwich,
I know they inherited the smell, tastes and memories
of their ancestors.

Why She's Unaware

She doesn't know her Damascus,
of storytellers in cafés,
of Blue Beach and Roman theatre
or any of its other features.

She hasn't walked along the banks of the Euphrates
or had tea with the Bedouin women,
visited the ruins at Serjilla
or ever smoked a *nargileh.*

She borrowed her knowledge of Syria
from television shows and tittle-tattle,
doesn't fully understand the tradition,
simply follows the shepherd's cane like a sheep.

One day she will fly from here to there,
to live amongst the locals,
drink tap water, unpasteurized milk,
perhaps wear a veil as she tells a stranger *"Ahlein."*

Only then can she know the truth
and honestly compare,
be authorized to declare
what's considered beautiful and ugly over there.

My Company

Now that I'm alone,
the laughter opens its wings and flies away.
Our fun is fun but also temporary.
Soon I'll be in my room, lying in bed without a man,
my hips and breasts clothed,
the mattress on my left side never worn.
Nights, whatever I've eaten earlier will soothe me,
put me to sleep like a pill.
Mornings, an alarm clock will wake me,
pouring me out to the world like an oil spill:
Widow, Daughter, Sister, Aunt, Friend,
Student of Earth
Example of Obedience
Teacher of Patience
An Observer of Life
But not a Lover.
I want to be the girl with the diamond ring,
no longer the one carrying all those profound titles
over her conscience, preventing her from
living the life of her dreams.

Progress Trap

The world is neon-pink,
loud with wanting and competition
and hard like a ceramic dish,
accumulating hotter issues everyday
as innocence faces extinction,
is barbecued like the dinosaurs.

My mother tells me stories of her past,
of her early years of marriage in Baghdad–
five decades ago–
when she lived in one house with
five other families.

"Oh, those were the days," she sighs,
recalling how well people treated each other back then.
"It wasn't like today, where husbands and wives
can't live under one roof!"

Expecting

I brought blank paper and a sharpened pencil
to the playground in the hope that I could
splash a bit of creativity
onto my soul, by composing a poem
while my three-year-old makes use
of the swings and slide.

However, it hasn't worked out quite the
way I planned. It's not like
preparing a bowl of *tabbouleh* or slicing
watermelon with Spanish cheese, making Turkish coffee
and serving it with sesame biscuits to dear guests.
No, this is not the same.
It's motherhood.
There isn't a lot of room
for lyrics and sonnets.

She keeps calling me to push her on the swing,
watch her go down the slide
and observe the sticks she has picked
off the ground.
When she's not shouting "Mom!"
I look up to make sure she's alright.

I Am a Mute Iraqi with a Voice

The situation is not as tense as it may sound.
Given the circumstances,
I've been able to write quite a few
lines in a short period of time.
I can't complain, really,
although, I wonder . . .
How will things turn out with the arrival
of the new baby
I expect to deliver
eight weeks from now?

What I Remember About Paris

We were stupid, my friend and
I, to have imaged that we could
take a one-day tour of Paris,
to think that the city known for its
fashion, food and art
could be enjoyed in a morning and a night.

The city's women wore colors,
not necessarily matching:
blue, purple, green and orange.
It was November but many had on open-toe
high heels, combined with sleeveless shirts
and cashmere scarves.

The Eiffel Tower was around the corner
from where our tour bus stopped.
We took a few pictures there,
ate an overpriced lunch at a local restaurant,
were treated very nicely by the Parisians,
couldn't understand why,
since we were Americans
and expected to be hated there.

On the train ride back to London,
we realized the secret to why

I Am a Mute Iraqi with a Voice

we were treated so decently.
The French were smart enough
to tell from the texture of our
hair and the color of our skin
that we were, by blood,
Semitic or Mediterranean.

Race—sometimes it works for you
and you get served ice cream.
Other times, it works against you
and a death sentence is delivered to your door.

A Letter Addressed to Me

When I was you, I didn't understand what it meant to immigrate, the impact it would have on you and me. You left Baghdad, Iraq, at age nine, and that particular day stirs no recollection in your memory. It was all done secretly, so as to not raise the suspicion of Saddam's regime. You did not know what was ahead, except for a faraway mysterious place that people called "the U.S.A."

Although you were a minority in Iraq, a Christian, you didn't recognize how deeply your roots were anchored to its soil, as a Mesopotamian, a Neo-Babylonian. You didn't imagine you would in America learn of your identity and that's exactly what happened to me.

I never forgot you, your happy and well-balanced childhood. When I left you, you were a shy elementary student in Baghdad who walked to school dressed in a uniform, the sweet silence of the city and the smell of jasmine surrounding you. Twenty years later, I returned to rediscover your footprints. They were everywhere but not as full of peace and pleasantry as in the olden days.

While I was gone, your country had gone through two heart-wrenching wars and nine years of grueling sanctions. Your people were not the same but rather sad and tired, although nowhere as horribly affected as they are today. I felt guilty to have long ago escaped this cruelty to move to the land of freedom and opportunity.

By the end of my visit, I realized you were no longer in that country. You had lived only in my memory. I returned to my home in America and suddenly I let go of the former reality, of you. But recently you have returned to me, through my daughter, now age three. You and she are so much alike, only she is not as shy as me but the opposite, like her father and her outspoken western birth country.

The combination of you and her makes me see my mother in me. When soap suds fill my hands over the kitchen sink, or when I fry meat and tomatoes in a skillet and serve my husband after he returns from a hard day's work, I see my past, as I watched my mother do this over thirty years ago. And I realize that despite the generational gap—my mother being 40 years older than I—despite my having a career and my mother being illiterate; despite living in an English-speaking Christian country whereas my mother raised you in an Arabic-speaking Muslim country; despite me having traveled the world and my mother having barely left her habitat; a woman is a woman and a daughter is a daughter and a mother is a mother, whatever land she's on, whatever religion constitutes her life, whatever her educational level may or may not be.

Earthenware

My best friend bought me a gift,
something small, which I could lift.
An earthenware.

I stuffed it to the top with potpourri,
placed it on the table, it was free.
A scented earthenware.

It was white with blue lines and orange kisses
"Like the Iznik Turkish jug, dated 1580's."
A history-defined earthenware.

It lived in my house for years,
accumulated very little dust, received no sneers.
A respectable earthenware.

One afternoon it was grabbed by angry fingers,
thrown against a cupboard where the dent still lingers.
A memory-bound earthenware.

Amongst other things,
the anger had my best friend's name on it.
So *inkisar al-shar,* evil was broken, by it.
A foreseeing earthenware.

The Five of Us

The garden room in the non-smoking section,
where plants hang and windows are plenty,
is where the five of us don't like to sit.
It's far from the salad bar,
not near the crackers and chicken and broccoli soup.
Far from the macho cook who's happy to see us,
from the heavy waitress who often scares us.
Far from the entrance and exit doors
where people come and go
as we observe and ridicule,
get cozy and silly together in our booth,
like teenagers, only less youthful, wiser
no, not wiser, just more responsible.

Our Bride

If she says "yes,"
wraps our conditions around her like tulle,
we'll take the whole clan,
go knocking on goldsmiths' doors.
The bargaining will be partly humorous, partly cruel.

She'll get patted on the cheek,
blessed and fussed over.
Her package deal will include
ceremonies tightly compressed, like a garlic clove.
Hopefully no family members will feud.

We'll start with the *kilma,* word of promise,
followed by the *khetouba,* engagement.
At the *fersha,* the bed spread ceremony
that blesses the couples' intimate moments,
we'll throw a baby on the bed,
preferably, if available, a boy, to help prophecy
the sex of the baby expected to proceed.

The custom of henna will follow,
the wedding will be next.
The welcome-home from the honeymoon
is how it'll all temporarily end.

My Power Song

The sun awakens me,
gives me energy.
She is my daughter.

The sky calls upon me,
calms me.
He is my son.

The breeze comes at the right time
to shift me in the right places.
He is my husband.

The flowers surround me,
different colors—my favorite, orange.
They are my tribal family.

I make soup every day.
It is my writing.

Daily, Birth and Death are a part of me.

My Sunshine's First Day of School

She wakes up in the dark.
"Is it time to go to school?"
"No, sweetheart . . .Go back to sleep until morning comes."

She peeks out the window, sees the break of dawn.
"Mom, look! It's morning!"
I insist she return to bed.

We're in class, digital cameras and videos side-by-side.
I listen to the teacher describe what my first child
will soon experience. Lots of fun she will have.

She is so enthralled I no longer exist in her eyes,
the exact opposite of what I feel.
I cannot get my eyes off of her.

All I see is the day she was born,
the tears that formed inside of me
when they placed her by my head.

Four and a half years have passed.
The day I had looked forward to has arrived.
I will now have some free time on my hands.

I observe from a distance my "bigger than life"

I Am a Mute Iraqi with a Voice

daughter whom I named, in Arabic, Sunshine,
and thank her for having taught me the lessons
necessary for a genuine life.

A Waitress and a Nun

My daughter wants a bowl of soup
and I would do anything for my daughter
but make a bowl of soup when all I want to do is
spend a long time under a blanket coop
and not move. I want to be lazy for once,
to not be asked to do a thing.
Being a mom is being a 24-hour
waitress and nurse and teacher and nun.

What a Morning

I wake up early,
have a number of things to be angry about,
first and foremost, my all-day morning sickness
as I try to make it to my nine-o'clock assignment
at a convent, an interview with Mother Superior.

My uncle's wife, who's staying with us,
has screwed up our dinner, the broad beans
I had soaked in the pot overnight.
My two-year-old keeps tugging at my legs
for apple juice and pancakes.

Take a left turn as soon as you leave home,
I remember the directions.

I take a deep breath and promise to get some rest
during this one-hour drive to the convent.
Soon enough I will be the mother of two
little children.

A Season's Breeze

Goodbye, humming bird.
It's late autumn
and you must leave.

Without a winter coat
or enough oil on your skin
you will freeze.

I admire you
for understanding your needs
but that's common in your breed.

Blue jays and robins
migrate to the south,
unconcerned of who stays here.

I'll watch you,
model your ability to respect
how you inwardly feel.

A Step Backward to Move Forward

I want to bathe in milk
like Cleopatra
and the Lebanese entertainer Sabah
who at seventy odd years
still sings
and has a svelte figure.
Her most recent marriage was to a twenty-four-year-old
man, a Mr. Lebanon.

I want to wear an orange veil,
a crown of flowers, yellow shoes
like ancient Roman brides.

I want to bake fish I caught in the Nile
and do my laundry in that river too
without being bitten by a crocodile.

Be a priestess or a goddess,
eat kidney, pigeon stew.

I want to love, half-naively, half-smartly.
No matter, as long as completely.
No questions, or all questions, asked
No matter, as long as sincerely.

He and I

He knew me first
before I even knew me.
He loved me first
stronger than I even loved me.
Then he disappeared
like a peppermint,
leaving behind the smell and taste of his memory.
But where is he?
Are there women for him in heaven
or must he, up there, live like me?

The Idea of Positivity

Snow bakes under the sun outside my home.
A neighbor shovels the driveway.
It sounds like mushrooms sizzling in a pan.
The wooden chimes I bought on my honeymoon
do an exotic dance.
My daughter stirs my heart as she sleeps.

I finish cleaning.
I am almost ready for a nap
when a thought comes to me.
It's time to say something beautiful about my life.

For years, war stories have surrounded me
and for years, war stories will surround me,
but right now, I will take joy in observing
the white snow outside my door.

There are other topics in my life,
full of love and peace: the blue sky;
the orange, white, and black kittens recently born
under my porch;
the red bird that comes back despite the cold.
The squirrel too.

Today, I look away from negativity.

My Pencil

My yellow pencil sharpener is gone
although I've made sure lately
to place it in my pink zipper pouch that says KIDS,
the one made in France.

My credit cards and state ID are kept together
by a rubber band.
Scrunchies and un-sharpened pencils
are scattered in my purse.
I have a 2009 planner that I use to keep my life intact.
My daughter uses it for her scribbles.

I have no time to get
my specialty coffees from Caribou anymore.
Rather, I must order my lattes and mochas
from McDonald's drive-through window.

I have several stops to make once
I've finished writing this poem:
tomorrow family is coming over for
New Year's Eve.
I must buy turkey gravy and diapers
and order a tray of shish kabob.

I miss you, paper, and I don't know

I Am a Mute Iraqi with a Voice

when I'll see you again in the form
of friendship, not as an
advertisement or a bill.

Goodbye, but we will meet again.

A Memory of Mother

In praise of sleeping next to my mom,
I remember the way my cold feet would slip
between her white, warm thighs.
The bedcovers were soft,
the house quiet but for our
breathing. The air crisp and I, safe.

That memory represents the way my mother
kept us strong and together. She was the tent,
protecting us through our various experiences,
maintaining relationships between siblings as
if none of us had ever moved out of the house.

For years, I've longed to sleep next to my mother
in that same way, and I'm jealous
when I hear that my niece, her grandchild,
snuck into her bed at night.
I want to do just that, if only once,
to smell her scent, even if it's full of Vicks and
the cream I bought for her from the Chinese doctor
to help remove her headaches.

I want to hear her breathe and
watch her sleep, the way she once
stared at me when I slept,

I Am a Mute Iraqi with a Voice

the way I now stare at my children.

I don't care if she shows approval or criticizes.
I just want to be in the same room with her.

Traveling Abroad Without Leaving Town

By accident, I land into this or that festival,
listen to a guitarist singing in Spanish, French, or Arabic
or view the artwork of a painter who brings to life the
Greek islands I once visited.

Tears run down my face
as I recall places and days I may never visit again.
At least, never in the same way.

My feet wander towards Paris.
I was not that young
nor was it long ago.
But I am not the woman I once was.
Today, I am a wife and mother.
I travel to Paris, Madrid, or Casablanca
through foreign songs,
not by airplanes.

There is no need to be sad.
I can explore the adventures of traveling
while staying in my neighborhood.
It's just a much shorter trip, that is all.

Both Without Teeth

If not for the wrinkles,
the dry skin on the soles of her feet,
the tight wedding band
bought in the forties by my dad
from a jeweler in the souk...

If not for the large breasts that long ago were potato-size,
the belly that once cradled child after child,
grocery bag after grocery bag,
as her veil flared against her ankles
in the souk...

If not for the way she spoke about old times
and cooked recipes from her homeland of Iraq,
and to go even further back, her village of Telkaif,
and to go even further than that, her Mesopotamia,
you'd see that she switched roles over time.

She has turned as soft as butter
is now without teeth,
dependent on others,
like a baby.
She handed down to me the role of a mommy.

Sense and Humor

My sense of humor is gone,
where to, I'm not sure.
I still laugh but can't come up
with any jokes.
I think I am, like everyone else, exhausted.

Can I return to my mother's womb
and start all over again?

Before We Get Married

Let's promise each other
to realize the beauty of our
time together and not waste it
arguing until, little by little,
we start to bicker about who
neglected to fill the sugar container,
dropped their dirty clothes on the floor,
and didn't turn off the living room lights
before going to sleep.

Let's promise to recognize the
importance of the two of us having
an outing alone rather than getting
caught up in the Middle Eastern web of attending
family functions, inviting such and such persons
to our home, and all the other duties
that are associated with being part of extended families.

Let's promise to not allow work to be
the full focus of our family
or to permit a sister or brother to meddle
in our affairs, or, once we have kids,
to forget that we are still a couple
capable of having a romantic dinner
without a baby's cry, a toddler's demands

Weam Namou

and spilled apple juice all around our plates of
stuffed grape leaves.

Let's promise to remember these vows,
and once a month, over cups of tea,
coffee and milk, adjust them to our realities,
to continue with that list
until the day we pass away
and forever merge together as spirits
yet become to the world a mere memory.

Similarities

She, with the option to go out and date,
wants to be alone,
a virgin, sole owner of her body,
her mind,
her heart.
And I, desperate to share,
to give my body
my mind, my heart
have no option but to be alone.
Yet her words are, "I want to find someone."
Mine are, "I am content."

Dear Mother

When I had my first contraction,
I thought, dear Mother, how did you
give birth to twelve?

When I couldn't have a moment's peace
as my colicky daughter cried buckets of tears,
I thought, dear Mother, how did you
ever have a chance to eat?

When I changed six to seven diapers a day,
I thought, dear Mother, how did you find the
time to wash so many pieces of cloth?

When I played with my daughter,
chasing her around the house,
I thought, dear Mother, were you
ever non-pregnant to physically do that?

And when I kiss my two children's cheeks and
run my fingers over their soft skin,
thanking God for such blessings,
I can't bear to think how you felt
when you lost your first-born.

My Little Woman

Two years have passed
and I still don't recognize the person
she has turned me into.
Who is she, this little woman
who half the time calls me mom,
half the time calls me by my first name?
Who is this little woman who barely
comes up to my calves and yet commands
me as she pleases, as if she were my boss,
has me wrapped around her finger
like the wedding ring I wear!
I look at her and see how worthless
my own thoughts often could be–
how unnecessary it is to hold onto
the past and not live in the moment,
like she.

My Brother

When I was twelve,
he was twenty-one
but now that I'm an adult,
I feel like he's my son.

I pray each time I see him dress,
splash on cologne, start the car,
tell his friends, *I'll be around.*

I imagine the scene of loud music, cigarette smoke,
of liquor and hearts that are broke
as he checks out the girls who wink and stare
and walk around revealing everything they possess,
without a sense of self.

I am certain he reflects on his life
and I say, God, help him find his type,
she who will love him unconditionally,
and be his wife.

She will give him the energy to embrace
the things of his ancestors –
God, love, family, community
which he tries to unnaturally replace.

The Mistress

She is the sun,
shining everywhere
but remaining out of reach.

She is the shore,
embracing oceans and debris
without a cry or a reply.

She is the grain,
feeding people and birds,
gentle as a feather.

She is the wind,
welcoming strangers,
strangers who'll ask questions, inspect.

She is the fire,
consuming suitors and rejections,
without shame or tragedy.

She is the mistress,
waiting to be understood by someone,
whom she'll call the man of her dreams.

Original Birth

Had I grown up on the beach,
would I still have made myself, to men, out of reach?
Would my flesh have been forbidden
or each and every curve of it been enjoyed, eaten?
Would I have resisted, frowned upon, their hungry stares,
or encouraged them, as long as they were not snares?
Would I have hidden between rocks and clams
or flip-flopped in a fisherman's hands?
Could I have slipped back into sea
or shared the company of thee?
Would I like to have that type of birth
or am I comfortable in my curse?
Or is it not a curse at all,
but a question of perception overall?

PART IV

Animals and Vegetables

At the Dog Mall

My cousin and I took the children to an outdoor mall where pretty and fancy dogs prowled around.

Our children dipped their hands and hair in the fountains, reaching for the coins that those with wishes had thrown.

Coins started to circle our feet, fingerprinted with the desires of someone wanting to get married, another to be rich, or wishing for citizenship.

We fed the children ice cream and chips, changed them into dry clothes, watched them pet the dogs, and stopped them from riding the animals as if they were stallions.

By the time we returned home, I was six hours closer to my due date and truly exhausted. I wondered where the day had gone.

Before marriage, I lived in my mother's home as Arab tradition goes, where my mother prepared my meals and did my laundry, though I had plenty of responsibilities.

I Am a Mute Iraqi with a Voice

Now, chasing a toddler, another baby in my belly, I felt
that woman I once knew is nowhere to be found.

Should I just bury her and bring to life someone else,
or wait for her to come back?

Then again, did I really want her around?
Probably not, I decided,
recalling how I had once prayed to be where I was now.

Diego by the Pool

A pool party,
the 4th of July,
no fireworks;
Diego, the black cat, is outside.
The heat so strong,
the water nice and cool,
children playing, enjoying a swim,
eating pizza and chicken wings,
drinking soda pop and lemonade
when a scream interrupts everything.

"Diego is trying to eat the bird!"

A struggle to release Diego's teeth
from the baby bird's wings,
yet it's too late.
A wound is made,
blood is spotting on the floor.

The mother screeches frantically,
flies from tree branch to fence post.
My brother picks up her offspring,
carries it somewhere "safe"
where she, the mother, can get to it.

I Am a Mute Iraqi with a Voice

A question is raised:
"What could the mother do anyway?"
Someone responds: "Nothing."

Diego, locked inside,
keeps his face pressed
against the kitchen's glass door,
wants more. To kill.

Brother is baffled. "I didn't know cats still did that."
Everyone laughs.
I want to ask, "What, you thought they've evolved,
when humans have not?"

Planting Life

On my morning walk,
I see what my neighborhood's people have grown:
red and black raspberries, pears, apples.
I pick and eat
and imagine perhaps next year
having a garden of my own,
planting tomatoes, cucumbers
and jalapeno peppers.
I would place my hand beside
that of my young daughter,
and we would touch the same
soil that would help us
create a different life, a spiritual fate.

The Polish Rooster

Days pass like nightmares.
Fruits have no taste.
Not even watermelons and honey.
Awaiting change.
How can I flip my mood, my terrible attitude?
Where is the faith that keeps a child solid?
Why do adults feel lost in their lousy desires? Why . . .
      A rooster crows!
In the suburbs? That's odd.
Suburbs are meant for cats and dogs, perhaps birds and hamsters...
      A rooster crows!
Again?
For a moment the heart surrenders to long-ago days, when
I was a child,
a stranger to frustrations
in the city of Baghdad . . .
      A rabbit jumps up in front of a pear tree
      and with all its might, takes off.
A rabbit and a pear tree!
How peculiar.

It's bedtime, when wives and husbands share their day's events

and trials.
I bring up the crowing rooster.
He responds, "Many Poles live in this neighborhood.
They raise animals."

I am touched, recalling my parents'
Christian village of Telkaif in northern Iraq
which is no longer inhabited by its natives
as they have been pushed out,
massacred,
by other religions and ethnicities.

I am grateful to be here, safe and sound,
to be alive!

Like Prophets and Saints

Like prophets and saints, the skunk is misunderstood.
He's a harmless little fellow,
as long as you respect his space.
Fearless, he gets out of no animal's way.
Peaceful too, moving slowly and calmly to and fro.
He only sprays as a last resort.
But first he gives a warning, some clue.
His squirts are accurate, but not lethal,
can easily be removed with tomato juice.
So, either don't disrespect his turf
or don't worry too much after he gets you good.
Not everything that your body, or mind,
comes in contact with
has to smell of sweet perfume.

Termites

Termites destroy wood and the structure of your home,
that's true, but they're one of the few insects that are edible
to me and you.

High in protein, they're many animals' treats,
a great delicacy in Africa and the Middle East.

A boon to plants, they turn wood into a powder
that creates nitrogen, from which fertilizer is made.

Producers of methane gas: it stops oxygen
from becoming more than the right quantity for our survival.

Yet, no one here really gives a hoot about termites.
They're given the backseat to cupcakes and donuts.

Pomme

What do they call an apple in France?
Pomme, and do you know why?
They know its origin.
The apple grew out of a bush, the hawthorn tree.
The thorn tree is pretty in spring, its blossoms nice
but it can't be eaten.
All its parts are poisonous.
So people got rid of the thorns and created the crab apple.

The apple is not that old.
They depict it as though it was always here,
since biblical times.
It wasn't always here.
There's a theory that it was the tomato,
a fig or the pomegranate that got Adam and Eve
kicked out of Eden.

The apple is good.
But they depict it as though
Allah Himself made it, and that's what's bad.

A Butterfly

"A butterfly lays its eggs in apple blossoms
and the worm eats from the core out.
That's where it matures and turns into a butterfly.
But I flip the moth off so it doesn't ruin the
fruit or vegetable."

"So you spoil its birth?"
I ask the Native American telling me this.

"The extent of me having spoiled it is worth it
when you eat the crops."

"Aside from insects, what else attacks the crops?"
I ask the Native American telling me this.

"People."

Fish

The smell of eggplant and cauliflower
overpower the sweet perfume I sprayed
all over my neck.
I've spent quite a bit of hours
cooking rice and stew
and defrosting fish for
my husband who decided that, this Lent,
he will abstain from meat.
There are worse addictions to fast from,
I think, but keep my thoughts to myself, sort of.

I want to blurt them out to tell the truth,
to express my real thoughts, but I love him
and so it's alright.
I will smell like fish and seafood.

Spring is Here

Spring, the warming of the land by the sun, is
when the ice recedes and melts into the ocean,
the earth turns on its axis, the hills and grass turn
from yellow to green, and the ewes have given birth.

Ewe's milk, cheese and clarified butter with spices
were not found in grocery stores but sold door-to-door
by the Bedouins who raised cattle.

Spring is new life
Summer is growth
Autumn is the fruits
Winter is the resting period

Days could be that seasonal, from morning until night.

HERMIZ PUBLISHING, INC.
Pick up a copy of Namou's other books:

www.ingramcontent.com/pod-product-compliance
Lightning Source LLC
Chambersburg PA
CBHW030602020526
44112CB00048B/1181